IMAGES
of America

THE BUFFALO
NAVAL PARK

The Buffalo Naval Park footprint has dominated the Buffalo Riverfront since 1977 when USS *The Sullivans* and USS *Little Rock* arrived from Philadelphia. Since its establishment, the park moved to make way for more development. This image shows the original configuration of the park from 1977 to 2003. After 2003, all the artifacts and ships moved downriver about 1,000 feet to allow for the growth of the historic Canalside district. Many people who visit mention they remember when USS *The Sullivans* was "under the Skyway," as evidenced by this photograph. While this image is undated, it does offer a nice and detailed overview of the park pre-2003.

ON THE COVER: USS *Little Rock* bristles in her original Cleveland-class configuration while the crew enjoys some sun on their way to South America. Looking aft from the bow, the two triple 6-inch/47-caliber guns and the waist-mounted twin 5-inch/38-caliber guns are clear. The Cleveland class was second to the Ticonderoga class in number of ships constructed. Twenty-six were completed while one was halted near completion. These had extended ranges and carried more anti-aircraft (AA) armament than prior light cruisers. USS *Little Rock* was in service as a Cleveland class from 1945 to 1949.

IMAGES
of America

THE BUFFALO
NAVAL PARK

Shane E. Stephenson,
Director of Museum Collections

ARCADIA
PUBLISHING

Copyright © 2023 by Shane E. Stephenson
ISBN 978-1-4671-0979-6

Published by Arcadia Publishing
Charleston, South Carolina

Printed in the United States of America

Library of Congress Control Number: 2023903149

For all general information, please contact Arcadia Publishing:
Telephone 843-853-2070
Fax 843-853-0044
E-mail sales@arcadiapublishing.com
For customer service and orders:
Toll-Free 1-888-313-2665

Visit us on the Internet at www.arcadiapublishing.com

*This book is dedicated to all the servicemen and women who chose
to enter the military. It is also dedicated to the men and women
of the shipyards who built the four vessels we proudly display.*

CONTENTS

ACKNOWLEDGMENTS

First and foremost, I wish to thank Paul Marzello, president and CEO of the Buffalo Naval Park. USS *The Sullivans* had her darkest and most precarious moments in 2022. Under Marzello's leadership and guidance with the Unified Command, she also had her brightest. The board of directors worked tirelessly through a trying year to keep staff morale positive and to retain our connections with the community while continuing to secure funding to fulfill the Buffalo Naval Park's mission. I'm sure the staff of the naval park got sick of me saying, "I'm working on the book!" I thank them for their patience. It also needs to be mentioned that all the staff worked very long hours and weeks under extremely stressful conditions. They all showed a passion for the job they do, and all pulled up their bootstraps! I'd like to acknowledge Dale Saeman and Jessica Nantka for helping me develop the primary arrangement of the photograph collection. I want to acknowledge the continuing support of the museum ship and Historic Naval Ship Association communities. They came to us as a unified front to ask how they could help, and they haven't stopped asking yet. Gabriel Dunn from unDunn Art Services was instrumental in helping me organize and preserve USS *The Sullivans* artifacts; I can't thank her enough. Lastly, I'd like to acknowledge our strong and supportive social media community, especially our YouTube subscribers. They reached out to us throughout the year asking how best to assist, making financial contributions, and stepping up to volunteer when we put out the call.

Unless otherwise noted, all images are courtesy of the Buffalo Naval Park archives.

INTRODUCTION

In 1940, US shipyards built 250,000 displacement tons of ships for the US Navy. Three years later, these same shipyards were building 2.5 million displacement tons of ships for the war effort. World War II is a case study of overwhelming one's enemy with war materiel, and America's industry produced at such a pace for the two-ocean war that it was only a matter of when the Axis powers would fall. This rapidity of shipbuilding and how it staggered the Axis powers is shown best in the number of fleet carriers built for the Pacific theater. America's fleet carrier production during the war, represented by the Essex and Independent classes, totaled 33 ships completed over the course of the war with a few under construction when the Japanese surrendered. Japan, by contrast, completed just five aircraft carriers throughout the war. America's wartime production was made possible through a private-public partnership between shipbuilders and the federal government. Across the nine private shipyards to receive public funding, including Newport News, Bethlehem Fore River, Bethlehem San Francisco, Cramp Shipbuilding, and Seattle-Tacoma Shipbuilding, they received 142 million federal dollars. Today, that sum is equal to $2.5 billion. Those funds allowed the shipyards to upgrade their equipment and docks after the relative quiet of the interwar period.

The Buffalo Naval Park's three tour-able vessels were constructed during this time, and as ships alone, they represent the ingenuity, engineering, and industrial might of the nation. But the ships are not just a mass of steel, wiring, welds, rivets, platforms, and decks; they also had active lives through which stories can be told. The Buffalo Naval Park's mission is to honor, educate, inspire, and preserve—to honor the ships and the men aboard while also honoring those from Buffalo and Western New York who served and sacrificed, to educate the public about what life in the Navy was like for the crew, to inspire the younger generations to take heed, and to use our artifacts while considering if serving in the military is right for them. Lastly, the park's mission is to preserve the artifacts in our care. USS *Little Rock*, USS *The Sullivans*, and USS *Croaker*, along with PTF-17, are the largest artifacts and deserve rightful attention, even when situations look dire.

Buffalo first saw the flames of war on December 30, 1813. The village of 500 residents was burned by the British army in retaliation for American forces burning the village of Newark just across the border in Ontario, Canada. Battles were fought across the Niagara frontier but mostly along the Niagara River, which separates America from Canada. Slowly, the village of Buffalo came back, and then it became a city at a crossroads. This time, the crossroads was of trade and commerce and not of soldiers carrying torches. Men and women of consequence from Buffalo left their mark on the US military, with names like Rear Adm. C. Wade McClusky, who pushed his scout bombers to the limit of their fuel capacity and led the American forces to the Japanese fleet at the battle of Midway, and William J. "Wild Bill" Donovan, known as the founding father of the Central Intelligence Agency. Gunnery Sgt. John Basilone, the only enlisted Marine to receive both the Medal of Honor and the Navy Cross during World War II, was born in Buffalo and learned to walk here before his family moved to New Jersey. More recently, Staff Sgt. David Bellavia was awarded the Medal of Honor for meritorious actions on November 10, 2004, in Fallujah, Iraq, while Cpl. Jason Dunham was also awarded the Medal of Honor, and a ship named for him, for meritorious actions on April 14, 2004, in Karabilah, Iraq. While people like Anna Mae Hays, the first woman to achieve the rank of general officer and brigadier general; Lt. Col. Matt Urban, one of the most decorated American soldiers of World War II who was awarded 12 personal decorations; Frank Gaffney, a Medal of Honor awardee who was considered the "second bravest man in the US Army" during World War I; and Albert James Myer, a surgeon during the Civil War and the father of the US Army Signal Corp and the US Weather Bureau, may stand out, they stand on the shoulders of the hundreds of thousands of military personnel who went about their duty without acknowledgment or accolades. You will meet some of these noble Buffalonians in this book.

The Buffalo Naval Park's three tour-able vessels also stand on the shoulders of all the men who manned them, fired their guns, lit their boilers, and protected America's interests during World War II and the Cold War. What this book will expose are some of the stories of those crewmen and the ships and equipment that helped them successfully complete their duty. When all was said and done with USS *Little Rock*, USS *The Sullivans*, and USS *Croaker*, they served a combined 69 years and traveled roughly seven million miles. Being the largest inland naval park in America raises a question—what does it mean to be the largest? Does "largest" represent square footage, amount of funding, or the most artifacts? The naval park is blessed with a diverse artifact collection, which can also be a curse if one thing goes wrong. After 2022 and the capsizing of USS *The Sullivans*, the park has many difficult questions to ask, including where to designate its limited maintenance funding to preserve the artifacts. For now, though, this book will explore the multiple pasts of the US Navy's people, places, and things.

One

BEGINNINGS

THE BUFFALO NAVAL PARK

CERTIFICATE OF DELIVERY AND ACCEPTANCE

This is to certify that pursuant to the terms of Naval Sea Systems Command Contract N00024-77-C-0202, the Officer in Charge, Inactive Ship Maintenance Detachment, Philadelphia, Pennsylvania, acting on behalf of the Secretary of the Navy, has on the 21st day of June 1977, at 1330 hours delivered and transferred possession of the obsolete destroyer ex-THE SULLIVANS (ex-DD-537) complete with installed machinery and contents (as is, where is) to the City of Buffalo, New York, at the berthing site at Philadelphia, Pennsylvania.

The undersigned, as the authorized representative of the City of Buffalo, has on said date and hour taken possession of said destroyer at the location indicated above and accepts delivery thereof in accordance with the provisions of said contract.

ACCEPTED: CITY OF BUFFALO, NEW YORK

By _Louis J. Clabeaux Jr._
LOUIS J. CLABEAUX, JR.

DELIVERED: UNITED STATES OF AMERICA

By _R. C. Clark_
CDR R.C. CLARK USN

Dated: _21 JUNE_ 1977

This certificate was the final step in the process that began in 1975 when Judge Anthony P. LoRusso visited Wilmington, North Carolina, and witnessed the positive energy a naval ship could bring to a waterfront. The certificate represents the signing over of USS *The Sullivans* to the City of Buffalo on June 21, 1977. Concurrently, a certificate of delivery and acceptance was also signed for the USS *Little Rock*. After the signing, USS *The Sullivans* began her 13-day journey from Philadelphia, arriving on Monday, July 4, 1977. She traveled up the Atlantic coast to the St. Lawrence Seaway, into Lake Ontario, and through the Welland Canal, which brought her into Lake Erie and on to Buffalo.

Getting ready for the St. Patrick's Day parade in 1978, dignitaries led by grand marshal Martha K. Hardin stand onboard USS *The Sullivans*. Once the ship arrived in Buffalo, it became an obvious gathering place for Irish people to show their pride. Hardin was the first woman to be grand marshal of the parade, and in later years worked to bring youth from war-torn Northern Ireland to Buffalo for summer vacations. They are standing below the banner that flew during the ship's towing from Philadelphia, visible in the following image.

Here, one of the transfer crew members who lived aboard USS *Little Rock* during her towing looks out from the starboard bridge wing. The lack of activity on the waterfront at the time of her arrival is evident. USS *Little Rock* arrived in Buffalo on Friday, July 15, 1977, and like USS *The Sullivans*, arrived under the cover of darkness. On Sunday, July 17, 1977, over 3,000 people gathered for the opening ceremony. It was attended by Jimmy Sullivan, son of Albert Sullivan, and his family.

With all three tour-able ships pier side, and the then-new home of the National Hockey League's Buffalo Sabres in the background, this image is dated between 1996 and 2003. The new home of the Buffalo Naval Park would incorporate the pier seen at lower left.

This is another overhead view of the original footprint of the Buffalo Naval Park. The parking lot and old museum building are now incorporated into the green space at Canalside, while the three ships are now tied up near the spot of the *Miss Buffalo I* and *II*, other longtime fixtures on the Buffalo waterfront. The pleasure craft are shown with striped awnings at lower right. Note that KeyBank Center, home to the Buffalo Sabres and Buffalo Bandits, has yet to be constructed, signifying this image was taken before 1996. At far left is the Buffalo Memorial Auditorium, home to the Sabres until 1995.

Here are the two ships coming to Buffalo. Above is the USS *Little Rock*, while below is USS *The Sullivans*. One of the major problems that faced the tug company and crew bringing USS *Little Rock* to Buffalo was the height of the ship. Two steps had to be taken to ensure her safe arrival. The first is very evident in this image: the main mast had to be cut in half. The mast, just forward of the black SPS-30 dish, has already been cut and laid on the deck of the 02, or second level. USS *Little Rock*, still height challenged, had to be flooded in parts of her bilge, voids, and second platform spaces to get her to rest deeper in the river. USS *The Sullivans* had no such problems.

The third tour-able vessel, USS *Croaker*, arrived to much fanfare in 1988, about 11 years after her sisters in the Buffalo River. The *Edward M. Cotter* fireboat can be seen spraying water, while two tugs begin positioning her next to the pier. USS *Croaker* was stricken from the Naval Vessel Register in 1971 and became a privately owned museum ship in Groton, Connecticut, where she was constructed in 1943. The private owner, Frank Scheetz, was a World War II submarine vet and local developer in Connecticut. He was able to secure USS *Croaker*, and in May 1977 opened

it to the public. Ten years later, with his capital and goodwill expended in an effort to get the USS *Nautilus* as a museum, the Navy clawed it back, with her last day as a museum ship on July 23, 1987. A little over a year later, this photograph was taken as USS *Croaker* arrived in Buffalo and began her long career as a museum ship here. In 2019, the Buffalo Naval Park celebrated her 30th year as a tour-able museum ship and expects she will be able to tell her story for many more years to come.

The original museum building was constructed in 1979, coinciding with the opening of the park to visitors. When the ships arrived in 1977, money was raised from various sources including Congressman Henry J. Nowak, who was able to secure $1.7 million for the naval park. The staff hired to bring the ships back to life took two years to show some "spit and polish" before allowing the first visitors onboard. The museum building housed exhibits, the ticket counter, and offices for the staff. A large atrium was able to show temporary displays, while along the edges of the building and the second floor, more permanent displays, artifacts, and wartime narratives were exhibited.

Here is the fourth vessel in the museum's collection while still commissioned. PTF17 is a Nasty-class fast patrol boat constructed by the John Trumpy and Sons Boat Builders out of Annapolis, Maryland, and was in commission for about 10 years. She saw action in Vietnam with special forces patrolling North Vietnam waters. After returning stateside, PTF17 became part of the 21st Coastal River Division based out of Chicago and patrolled the Great Lakes as part of the "brown water navy." This picture is from her service during that time. She arrived at the Buffalo Naval Park in August 1979 shortly after the grand opening of the park to visitors on June 30, 1979. Included in her are two 3,100-horsepower Napier Deltic engines. For armament she had one 40mm Bofor, two 20mm Oerlikons, and one 50-caliber. Eighteen officers and crew manned the ship during her service.

PTF17 is pictured above in need of repair after her 2003 move to the Buffalo Naval Park's new location, and below in her current stabilized state. In 2019, a veteran resource group comprised of workers from Northrup Grumman, Linde Air, and Home Depot set out on a three-year plan to solidify her hull, shore up the deck and bridge, and repaint. Her armaments have been scraped, primed, and repainted. She currently reflects the best preservation she has received in a long time. The Buffalo Naval Park has been appreciative of the work this veteran resource group has done and looks forward to continuing the work with resource groups in Western New York to preserve the other artifacts under its care.

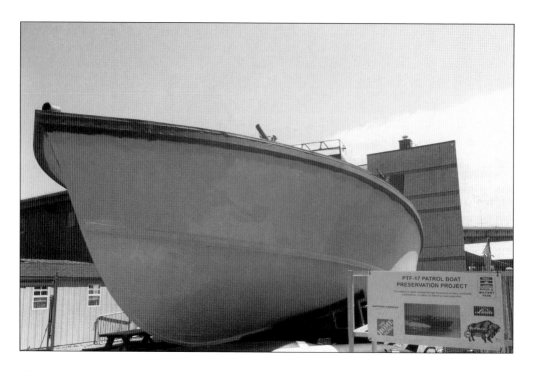

Here are two images of the F-101-F Voodoo jet tail No. 80338 currently on display in the yard at the naval park. The above image shows her on her last flight in 1982, and the image below shows her being towed for her final display very shortly after her last flight. She was transported to the Buffalo Naval Park over city streets and by barges. These planes, constructed by McDonnell, made their first test flights in 1954 and were put into service in 1957. In total, 785 of the F-101s were built. They had a maximum speed of 1,100 mph, with a cruising speed of 545 mph. The Niagara Falls Air Reserve Station accepted this and other Voodoos in 1971 for the 107th Fighter/Attack Wing unit stationed at the base. Currently, the plane is displayed on a pedestal and is of great interest to park visitors.

One of the most enjoyed displays at Buffalo Naval Park is the P-39 Airacobra hanging from the rafters in the museum building. This plane was flown by Lt. Col. William Shomo, who received the Medal of Honor for meritorious action when he attacked a squadron of overwhelming force and shot down seven Japanese planes during the melee. He later flew this plane, named *Snooks 2nd*, which was abandoned in New Guinea after World War II. It was salvaged, rescued, and repaired by Yesterday's Air Force, a company based in California. The final assembly took place in Buffalo after the plane's arrival in December 1980. It went on display in March 1981 in the old location, and as these two images show, was reassembled in 2007 at the new location. *Snooks 2nd* got its name from Shomo's crew chief, Ralph Winkel. It was a term of endearment Winkel used for his wife.

For many years at Buffalo Naval Park, the other jet on display was painted blue and gold in honor of the Buffalo Sabres. The decision was based on faulty information that led staff to believe the jet was a North American Aviation F-86 Sabre. For over 25 years, what was thought of as the F-86 Sabre was really an FJ-4 Fury. Both were constructed by North American Aviation, which eventually merged with Rockwell-Standard in 1967. The FJ-4 on display, tail No. 3610, is a later, sleeker design of the F-86, and there is a close "family" resemblance. As an all-weather interceptor, the Fury had to carry considerably more fuel, and had the ability to carry a nuclear weapon. The FJ-4 first went into service in 1955 and served until 1968. The image above shows the false color scheme, while the image below shows Seymour Knox, founder and owner of the Buffalo Sabres, second from left, along with Jim Schoenfeld, a defenseman for the Sabres, third from left.

In 1995, Buffalo Naval Park received a new artifact for display: a Nike Hercules missile and launch pad. This missile was being deaccessioned from Camp Smith in Peekskill, New York. These images show the crew that transported it from Westchester County. The missile and its predecessors were the product of a 1945 project to develop high-altitude, long-range air defense for the US mainland. It was eventually used by both American and NATO forces. The Hercules was an upgrade from the Nike Ajax missile, first put into service in 1954, four years before the Hercules. The Buffalo-Niagara region had seven Nike missile bases that ranged from Hamburg, New York, to Niagara Falls, New York. Taken together, these bases were in service from 1955 to 1970. The Nike Hercules represented the United States' primary surface-to-air missile until it was replaced in 1984 with the Patriot.

Two

USS LITTLE ROCK

HER TWO LIVES

This image of USS *Little Rock*, CL92, taken in 1945, shows the fantail of the ship in her original Cleveland-class cruiser configuration. With two planes mounted on catapults, the aft of the ship was used as the launch point for these Curtiss SC Seahawk reconnaissance floatplanes. First constructed in 1944, these planes, built by the Buffalo-based Curtiss-Wright Company, numbered about 600. Since they appeared late in the war, they were added immediately to later commissioned Cleveland-class cruisers like USS *Little Rock*. Posing for the pictures are four sailors on their way to South America. The two standing are third-class and second-class yeomen, and the two below, without insignia, may be seaman recruits or seaman apprentices, possibly fresh out of boot camp.

Here is USS *Little Rock* during her launching on August 27, 1944. She was constructed by the William Cramp & Sons Shipbuilding Company in Philadelphia and was the second-to-last ship built by the company for World War II. The last, USS *Galveston* (CL93), was nearing completion when work stopped, and she was put into the reserve fleet. USS *Little Rock's* keel was laid March 6, 1943, and along with USS *Miami*, USS *Astoria*, and USS *Oklahoma City*, were the four Cleveland-class cruisers commissioned for World War II from the Cramp Shipyard. The ship's sponsor, Ruth May Wassel, the wife of a Little Rock, Arkansas, alderman, smashed a bottle of champagne on the ship's bow, sending her down the ways to bring her one step closer to active service.

U. S. S. Little Rock

Commissioning Dinner

United States Navy Yard
Philadelphia

Here is the cover of the commissioning dinner booklet for USS *Little Rock*. When a ship is commissioned into the US Navy, it signifies that it is ready to be turned over to the branch for active use. The ship's life transfers from construction and sea trials to being ready to take on her crew and become part of the fleet wherever she is assigned. The date of USS *Little Rock*'s commissioning was June 17, 1945, roughly 10 months after her launching. Those 10 months were used to fit out her interior, parts of her superstructures above the main deck, and her armaments. Capt. William E. Miller was her first commanding officer, while the commissioning crewmembers are known as "plankowners." Historically, being part of a commissioning crew entitled the sailors to one of the teakwood planks when they left the ship.

After USS *Little Rock's* commissioning in June 1945 and her crew's shakedown training cruise in August 1945, World War II ended with the Japanese unofficial surrender on August 15. Instead of putting *Little Rock* into reserve, the US Navy kept her in commission, and her first cruise was to sail to various ports throughout South America. These two images are from that cruise. *Little Rock* left Newport, Rhode Island, on October 21, 1945, and returned to Norfolk, Virginia, on March 23, 1946. The image above shows some of the plankowners relaxing and "missing their sweethearts" as they dance to music on the main deck forward, while the photograph to the left shows a sailor named Hank, a third-class quartermaster, along with Hashmark, USS *Little Rock's* first ship mascot.

Below the shadows of the Curtiss SC Seahawks, USS *Little Rock* begins a time-honored ritual known by many names, such as crossing the line, equatorial baptism, or the shellback initiation. Regardless of the name, one thing is clear: it is not pleasant for those being initiated. Those sailors who have not crossed the Equator prior are known—with variations—as "pollywogs," while those who have are "shellbacks." The ceremony initiates the pollywogs into the mysteries of the deep over an evening and a day. There is an appearance by King Neptune and his court, including Davy Jones and Amphitrite, a sea goddess from Greek mythology. The pollywogs appear before the court and endure a series of embarrassing hazing rituals. After the ceremony, the pollywog becomes a trusty shellback, with a certificate to prove their worth and acceptance. While the ceremony has undergone changes over the centuries, it is still a point of pride and bonding between the crew of any ship in the Navy.

USS *Little Rock* pulls into Rio de Janeiro, Brazil, for the first stop in her goodwill tour. In the foreground are the administrative buildings of the port. This photograph was taken November 10, 1945, just five days after *Little Rock* crossed the equator. The standard armament for the Cleveland class is evident. Twelve 6-inch/47-caliber guns in four turrets, twelve 5-inch/38-caliber guns in six mounts, one fore and aft and four at the waist, along with 28 quad and twin mounted 40mm Bofors and 10 single 20mm Oerlikon anti-aircraft guns. The ships of the Cleveland class, like USS *Little Rock*, were known as light cruisers, as the largest armament onboard were the 6-inch guns. Ships known as heavy cruisers during World War II carried 8-inch/55-caliber guns, the best example during the war being the Baltimore-class cruisers.

Here is a nice stern image of USS *Little Rock* in an unknown but distinctly foreign port. Her modified and improved Measure 22 camouflage scheme is evident. The colors used for this scheme are Navy blue and haze gray, and it created a graded pattern that could mask the true distance of the ship from an enemy vessel. With most of the hull Navy blue, following a straight line away from midships, the haze gray would appear at the bow and stern, as seen here. This created a lower profile for an enemy tracking the ship. They could interpret that lower profile to mean a greater distance away, throwing off their targeting calculations. Below the two Seahawk seaplanes and the crane to raise the planes from the water are the gun tubs and platforms for the twin 40mm Bofor anti-aircraft guns.

Here are two views of *Little Rock* still in her World War II configuration. In the image above, she sails in the Cape Cod Canal, a 17-mile canal that allows vessels to bypass Cape Cod and the islands of Nantucket and Martha's Vineyard. The *Little Rock* has just passed the Sagamore Bridge, constructed from 1933 to 1935. The bridge is still in use today. Based on the leisure boats in the picture below, this image could also have been taken in or around Cape Cod. This front-on view clearly shows the two forward waist-mounted 5-inch/38-caliber guns, one on each side of the forward superstructure. Barely visible is the early radar. The SK-2 air-search radar at the top of the mainmast is the most readily identifiable, and directly below are the Mark 34 and Mark 37 gun directors, each used to collate and send enemy data points for the 6- and 5-inch guns, respectively.

Here are two images of the crew during *Little Rock's* 1945–1949 career. At right, the gang is resting and having a laugh as a crewman plays a harmonica in one of the 40mm Bofor gun tubs or platforms. As part of her original armament, *Little Rock* had 16 barrels of these quad Bofor guns spread across four different gun platforms. These anti-aircraft weapons could fire at a rate of 140 rounds per minute, with a range of about four miles. Below, a crewman stands proudly on the forecastle of the ship forward of the triple-barreled 6-inch/47-caliber gun turrets.

After being placed out of commission-in-reserve in 1949, USS *Little Rock* was converted in 1960 to a Galveston-class cruiser. One of six Cleveland-class cruisers to be converted with the US Navy's first guided missile system, she is seen here being recommissioned in 1960, as a young girl waves in the foreground. Three ships—USS *Galveston*, USS *Little Rock*, and USS *Oklahoma City*—were fitted with the Talos system while three others—USS *Providence*, USS *Topeka*, and USS *Springfield*—were fitted with the Terrier system. These six ships were divided into two classes, the Galveston and Providence classes, based on which guided missile system they carried. Also visible are the two Talos missiles and the associated SPG-49 tracking radars and SPW-2 dishes, trained at about 140 degrees relative to the ship. USS *Little Rock's* conversion took about three years, cost $14 million, and employed 70 draftsmen to complete at New York Shipbuilding Corporation.

These two images show the firing of the RIM-8 Talos missile off the Mark 7 launcher. Both are firing off starboard, and the upper image shows the SPG-49 radars pointed in the same direction. These large domes acquired and tracked the target. Working in coordination with the SPW-2 small guidance dishes above and below these domes, they worked to guide the missile to the target. Though these images appear to be from the same cruise, there is a clear giveaway. Above, the diamond-shaped SPS-2 3D search radar can be seen. The SPS-2 was mounted to two US warships during the Cold War, USS *Little Rock* and USS *Northampton*. This radar was later replaced by the SPS-30, the large black dish seen below. This change signifies that these two photographs are a couple of years apart.

Here is a close-up of the Talos missile firing. Of note from this angle is the basic gray on the deck of the fantail. By the late 1950s, helicopters had become an important military weapon platform. While USS *Little Rock* started receiving helicopters immediately, the black and white landing pad had not yet been painted on the deck. This view also shows the missile mated with its booster. Five seconds after launch, the booster decouples and falls away into the water as the ram jet, an air-ignited engine in the missile, fires up and takes over propulsion.

While the primary mission of USS *Little Rock* in the Mediterranean Sea was to show the flag, represent American interests, and keep the peace between countries, she also hosted many engagements and events for dignitaries and citizens of various countries. In these two pictures, taken during the same event, Kathy Bennet, the 13-year-old daughter of the commanding officer, conducts the US Sixth Fleet Band above, while they continue to play under the direction of the true band leader in the image below. The US Sixth Fleet Band was the Navy's largest sea-going band. Both images were captured on June 24, 1969.

In this undated photograph, Diana Petersen performs with the US Sixth Fleet band. This was a set show that was performed in the various ports around the Mediterranean, though where they are performing in this image is not known. Building positive relationships with countries during the Cold War was a necessary and important principle in establishing American influence around the globe. Post–World War II, many countries were caught in a political and ideological vacuum, with both East and West looking to gain influence. These concerts, along with offering tours of USS *Little Rock* to the citizenry of different countries, were a way of establishing relationships and increasing American influence. The caption on the back of this image reads, "The show travels throughout Europe bringing the international language of music to many foreign lands."

The overhead shot at right looking from the bow to the stern shows the various watercraft such as motor whaleboats and gigs that were stored on USS *Little Rock*. The boat decks were tucked away midships and stored various watercraft for the crew, commanding officer, and admiral when he was aboard. King posts and trackways lowered and raised the boats in and out of the water. From this picture, it appears that the admiral's barge is along the port, or left, side of the boat while four other boats occupy the starboard side. These may include the captain's gig, 40-foot personnel boats, and utility boats. This picture was taken while USS *Little Rock* was homeported in Gaeta, Italy, in 1968 or 1969. Below is a photograph of *Little Rock* from a liberty boat taken by crewman Louis Bykowski while speeding away from the ship.

Looking from the deck of the missile house, the stern of USS *Little Rock* is shown in rough seas. Two sailors are defying the weather and stabilizing themselves against the roll of the ship. USS *Little Rock* and her five sister ships were known as very top-heavy ships, with all the associated equipment added after World War II and their enlarged superstructures to host that equipment. The helicopter landing pad has not yet been painted on the fantail. At left is one of the SPG-49 guiding radars that track targets. With two Talos missiles able to be fired simultaneously, there was one SPG-49 radar dedicated to each missile.

Above, commanding officer Walter Bennet is meeting with four seamen and one fireman, all of whom were from Norwalk, Connecticut, and surprisingly served aboard USS *Little Rock* together. The image below shows the ship in spit-and-polish shape and the crew with officers and enlisted wearing their dress whites. The ship's yardarm is emblazoned with alphabet flags, while officers and crew gather on the 04-observation deck. Unfortunately, no information is listed about this ceremony, the location, or the year. The flag flying from the palatial building in the background may be the Egyptian or Syrian flag.

While receiving dignitaries and honored guests brings the ship to life as in the previous image, there is always room for liberty and recreational activities. These two images show some of the activities engaged in by the officers and crew aboard USS *Little Rock*. Above, the Tigers of USS *Little Rock* are engaged in a game of gridiron against the crew of USS *Independence* (CV62). *Little Rock* bested the team from the carrier, 14-6. The playing field is part of Carney Park, a US military recreational facility near Naples, Italy. Below is an image from the deck of the missile house—a boxing ring where the crew can take out their frustrations. In the background is a 40-foot personnel boat.

The above image shows a Kaman SH-2 Seasprite helicopter from Helicopter Support Squadron Four (HC-4). This squadron was commissioned on July 1, 1965, and eight years later assumed a new mission under anti-submarine warfare. Here, on the fantail of USS *Little Rock*, it may have participated in a vertical replenishment. Also of note is that its nose is detached and folded off to the side for maintenance. Below is another image of the crew and officers in what appears to be dress whites. The unknown ship where this photograph was taken seems to be receiving or sending dignitaries, officers, or crew in the double highline chair that is strung between both ships. The chair can be seen in the bow wave of the ship. The observation deck on the 04 level and the gun director platform on the 05 level are crowded with crew.

AN/SPS-42 RADAR ANT. ASSY.

MISS DIST & TELEMETERING ANT.

AN/SPS-2, RADAR ANT.

R/T ANT 11-3

(2) AN/SPG-49 RADAR ANT.

4

U.S.S. LITTLE ROCK (CLG4)
STBD SIDE LOOKING FORWARD
NEW YORK SHIPBUILDING CORPORATION
CAMDEN, NEW JERSEY
MAY 3, 1960

TACAN ANT., AN/SRN-6
D.F. ANT. 5-6, AN/URN-4

XMTG ANT. 2-4
28' HORIZ. WHIP
VHF ANT. 6-2
AN/SPS-17, RADAR ANT.

IFF ANT. 9-1
UHF ANT. 4-3 (OVER
UHF ANT. 4-1 (UNDE)

MK25 MOD. 3 RADAR AN
MK13 MOD. O
RADAR ANT.
VHF ANT. 6-3
URN. REFL.

A month before the ship's commissioning, this shipbuilder's photograph shows the antenna and radar arrays, modernized for the new threats of the 1960s and 1970s. The diamond-shaped AN/SPS-2 radar was only fitted to USS *Little Rock* and USS *Northampton*. As a height-finding radar, it tracked airborne targets. At the very top of the mainmast is the TACAN (tactical air navigation) system, used to gather the bearing and distance of targets. Most of the equipment topside on USS *Little Rock* was used for air search and surface search, extending the eyes of the ship over greater distances, and UHF antennas for communication with other ships in the fleet across many variable frequencies. Many radars of the Cold War era received information and transmitted it to computers onboard, which would resend that data to secondary radars and receivers. Each radar had specific ranges and elevations; some were two-dimensional, while others were three-dimensional. In concert, the myriad systems would construct an invisible shell around the ship by knowing where every bogey or friendly was at any given moment.

Cruises with family members were always a highlight of the crew's time at sea. USS *Little Rock* hosted family members many times during her service. These "Tiger cruises" were usually short transits from the last port of call to a ship's homeport. It was established by the Navy to help families gain deeper knowledge about what their crewman did and how they lived while they were out to sea. Here, the wives of two crew members, Doris Roye (left) and Tina Weyman, plot and track the movements of friendly contacts around USS *Little Rock*. Weyman wears a sound-powered phone headset, and they are set up in the combat information center, their husbands' duty station. During these cruises, many crew members would share the honorific "Dadmiral," a name given by their children.

The image above shows the decking of the missile house on the 02 level and one of the radio-controlled drones. Drones could be used as forward-deployed attack weapons or as targets for ships of the fleet to keep the gun crews in good practice. USS *Little Rock* carried and launched these drones, which were used as target practice by the other fleet ships. The image below shows a close-up of the Kaman SH-2 Seasprite on the fantail of USS *Little Rock*. The Seasprite was designed to meet the defensive and reconnaissance needs of the Navy: a compact, all-weather helicopter. They were 52 feet in length with a 44-foot rotor diameter. Primarily used for anti-submarine warfare due to their small size, they also conducted vertical replenishments for all ships of the fleet from aircraft carriers to destroyers.

At the USS *Little Rock* chow line is Gunner's Mate Chief Master Olene O. Henderson, who in 1969 was the force master chief for the commander in chief, US Naval Force Europe. In his position, he represented the interests of the thousands of enlisted men who served the Navy in the European and Mediterranean theater. Clearly visible is his rate badge along with seven service stripes near the cuff. Each stripe represents four years of naval service, signifying that Master Chief Henderson had served at least 28 years at the time. Below, Aerographers Mate 1st Class Peter P. Rend holds a weather balloon in the flag weather office on the 03 level. There is a family member of one of the crewmen peering in from the porthole during this 1965 Tiger cruise. This image came from the two adult children of Peter Rend when they visited the ship. Connecting with children of former crew members allows the Buffalo Naval Park to fill out its collections with diaries, images, and artifacts.

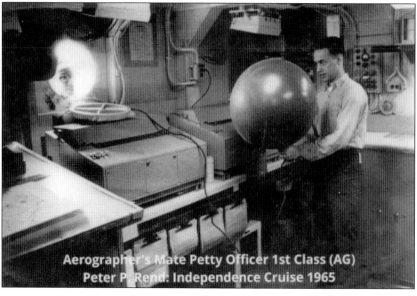

Aerographer's Mate Petty Officer 1st Class (AG) Peter P. Rend: Independence Cruise 1965

Here is a strange sight to those who did not know: USS *Little Rock* carried up to six cars and vehicles onboard; this Volkswagen Bus is from March 1972. The vehicles were carried on the deck of the missile house and were for the officers and crew. Glenn Gray, a crewman aboard the ship, was the driver for Vice Adm. William Martin from 1968 to 1970. The vehicles were craned off the ship when it was in port of calls or its home port in Gaeta, Italy, while in the Mediterranean. Below, the port profile image of USS *Little Rock* from January 1961 shows three vehicles under white covers next to the aft superstructure.

A volatile event during USS *Little Rock's* service was the USS *Liberty* incident. Occurring during the Six-Day War between Israel and Egypt, the USS *Liberty* was stricken by Israeli armed forces by way of a torpedo hit on the starboard side forward and strafing by Israeli jets. Thirty-four American sailors perished during the attack, and eight of the wounded were cared for in USS *Little Rock's* sick bay. It was no doubt clear that the ship was flying an American flag, so the admiral onboard *Little Rock* had serious questions for Israeli leaders. Other flagship duties were to protect the ship from further attack, to put the fleet into a defensive condition, and to triage the injured. This image shows the view of USS *Liberty* from the port side bow of USS *Little Rock*.

USS *Liberty* was an auxiliary general technical research ship (AGTR-5), and it had the ability to scan communications of other nations clandestinely. While the ship was a US naval vessel, it was under the control and purview of the National Security Agency and Central Intelligence Agency. Questions have continued to be asked regarding Israel's actions. Records show that Israel gave a warning to American forces that they would attack any vessel that was within 100 miles of their shore. At the time of the attack, USS *Liberty* was sailing between 14 and 25 miles from shore. Also, the aggressive action of attacking a ship of Israel's only ally raises other questions. Here is a close-up of the stricken ship showing a Seasprite taking off from, or landing on, the bow of the ship. It can be imagined the helicopter was bringing supplies and men aboard while carrying off the wounded or dead.

A USS *Little Rock* crewman enjoys a view of the ship while looking out over the Mediterranean at sunset. During her 17-year second commissioning, USS *Little Rock* was attached to fleet cruises in the Atlantic, Caribbean, and Mediterranean. It was home to countless thousands of enlisted crew, officers, and admirals. Today, when meeting with USS *Little Rock* sailors who come aboard her, one can hear the pride in their service. They stand a little bit taller, and there is joy on their faces as they talk to their children and grandchildren about their sacrifice. The Buffalo Naval Park is proud to be the home of the last remaining Cleveland, Galveston, or Providence class ship in the world. It is the park's mission and duty to continue to tell the story of this ship that protected America's interests around the world during the Cold War.

Three

USS *The Sullivans*
The Ship of Sacrifice

One of the most iconic images from World War II is this photograph of the five Sullivan brothers standing on the fantail of USS *Juneau* (CL52). Taken during the commissioning of the ship on Valentine's Day 1942, the ship would be lost nine months later almost to the day on November 13. From left to right are Joseph, Francis, Albert, Madison, and George Sullivan. George was the oldest at 27, and Albert was the youngest at 20. Both George and Francis had enlisted in the Navy prior to World War II and were rated higher than their three younger brothers. George was a gunner's mate second class, while Francis was a coxswain second class. Joseph, Madison, and Albert were all seaman second class, not yet experienced enough to have rates, though no doubt they each had been training for one during the ship's service. The Sullivan family experienced the greatest loss of any one American family during wartime.

In what may be the last picture taken of the Sullivan family together, this January 1942 image, shot at the family home at 98 Adams Street in Waterloo, Iowa, shows a smiling Alleta Sullivan with all her children. From left to right are (first row) Albert and his wife Katherine Mary (Roof) Sullivan, Alleta and Tom (holding nine-month-old Jimmy Sullivan), the boys' sister Genevieve, and Francis; (second row) George, May Abel (Alleta's mother), Madison, and Joseph. Though Albert was the youngest of the five brothers, he was the only one married and the only one to produce a child. Jimmy was less than two years old when he lost his father and uncles. From Jimmy and the children of Genevieve, the Sullivans' story thankfully continues to this day. (Courtesy of the Grout Museum District, Waterloo, Iowa.)

These two images, both from 1940, show the Sullivan family in happier times before the war. The image to the right captures, from left to right, Madison and Genevieve crouched on the ground below Pearl Schrader (a friend of Genevieve, holding a cat), Tom, Katherine Mary, and Albert. Below are Tom and Alleta, parents of the six Sullivan children. A moving story regarding images of the family taken before and after the boys' loss is Alleta's smile. It is said one can identify the date of any photograph of Alleta by her expression. Understandably, most images taken after the loss of her boys fail to show the smile she displays here. (Both, courtesy of the Grout Museum District, Waterloo, Iowa.)

These two images again show the pre-war smile of Alleta. The photograph above shows Alleta's involvement with the Navy Mothers Club of America, Yarnell No. 66. This local Waterloo chapter was named after Adm. Harry Yarnell, who hailed from Independence, Iowa, and was commander of the Asiatic Fleet just before the war. The Navy Mothers Club of America was established in 1930 as a charity and welfare club with chapters throughout the country. The image at left shows, from left to right, (first row) Francis and Joseph; (second row) Genevieve, George (puffing out his chest), and their mother. (Both, courtesy of the Grout Museum District, Waterloo, Iowa.)

These two images, taken in 1940, along with the others in this book, bring life to a family that most often is frozen in time around the frightful sinking of USS *Juneau* in November 1942. At right, Madison stands proudly in front of the American flag. Below, he poses playfully with his sister (left) and Pearl Schrader. Behind them is a glimpse of the late-Depression-era neighborhood where the family settled. The neighborhood was bracketed by the railyards where Tom Sullivan worked. A well-known story of the day Tom and Alleta were officially notified of their sons' loss is that Tom immediately left the house to start his shift. His railyard hauled war freight, and he coped with the news by doing his part to move it to the front lines. (Both, courtesy of the Grout Museum District, Waterloo, Iowa.)

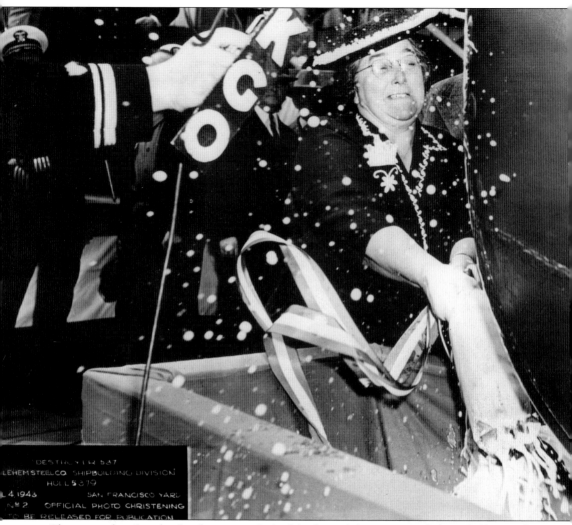

DESTROYER 537
LEHEM STEEL CO SHIPBUILDING DIVISION
HULL 5379
L 4 1943   SAN FRANCISCO YARD
N° 2   OFFICIAL PHOTO CHRISTENING
TO BE RELEASED FOR PUBLICATION

Three months after the family was notified of the loss of the *Juneau* and their children, Alleta smashed the christening bottle against the bow of USS *The Sullivans* at Bethlehem Steel's Shipbuilding Division Yard in San Francisco. The christening film shows a heart-wrenching moment. Ten seconds after this photograph was taken, as the ship was sliding down the ways, Alleta bowed her head in anguish and was consoled by an admiral and commander who came to her aid. She is seen wrapping her arms around them, not able to watch the ship that represents her boys and the cherished memories of them she carried with her.

USS *The Sullivans* slides down the ways in San Francisco. Originally constructed to be called USS *Putnam*, the name was changed to USS *The Sullivans* by order of Pres. Franklin Roosevelt to capture the moment and fighting spirit for a nation. One of 175 Fletcher-class destroyers constructed during the wartime building program, one of these Fletchers was sliding down the ways at America's shipyards every five days for 30 months. The image below shows the ship's emblem, a shamrock, painted on the fore funnel while in service. There were very few destroyers that were able to have their emblem emblazoned somewhere on the ship. Included with *The Sullivans* were USS *Kidd*, USS *Haywood L. Edwards*, USS *Mertz*, and USS *Cassin Young*.

On January 22, 1944, King Neptune and his court came aboard USS *The Sullivans* for the time-honored tradition of crossing the line. USS *Little Rock* crossed the equator on November 5, 1945, with much the same "services" shown in chapter two. Here are two images from the decks, above which flew the Jolly Roger pirate flag. At left, a member of King Neptune's court sits, watching a haircut being given to a blindfolded pollywog, while below are the results of the ceremony on the face and body of an unhappy sailor.

In a continuation of the equatorial ceremony, another pollywog is dunked in a tub of watery garbage mixed with other mysterious liquids. These ceremonies, which continue to this day, build esprit de corps among the crew. In the World War II era, they usually took place before the ship participated in combat. To this day, many sailors from the World War II and Korean era keep their trusty shellback certificates, signed by King Neptune and Davy Jones themselves, as a point of pride. In addition to crossing the equator, there are also Blue Nose ceremonies when crossing the Arctic Circle, the Special Order of the Guinea Pig for those who were present at the nuclear tests at Bikini Atoll, and Frozen Stiff for those who cross into the emperor penguins' domain by crossing the Antarctic Circle. Sailors could also become a "mossback" by going around stormy Cape Horn, and a "golden dragon shellback" by crossing the International Date Line. These certificates play a role in telling the story of sailors and what they experienced during their service.

After crossing the equator and fitting out at Pearl Harbor in late 1943, USS *The Sullivans* was off to join the Pacific fleet attached to fast carrier task forces TF38 and TF58. Here are two images during wartime. Above is a full side perspective of the ship showing the well-known profile of the Fletcher-class destroyers. This was near Ponape Island, between the Marshall Islands and New Guinea. The five 5-inch/38-caliber gun mounts are present, and the Mark 37 gun director is on top of the bridge. The antennae, facing aft, are the Mark 12 and 22 antennae first fitted on the Fletchers. Over time, as threats and technology changed, many Fletchers, including USS *The Sullivans* and museum ship USS *Cassin Young*, changed over to a Mark 25 radar dish. USS *Kidd*, also a museum ship, still has the Mark 12 and 22 mounted, as she closely resembles her World War II configuration with very little modification. The image below, though a little washed out, shows USS *The Sullivans* making a large rooster tail wake.

This startling image comes from USS *The Sullivans* photographic collection at the Buffalo Naval Park, but there is no description other than listing *The Sullivans* as the ship in the photograph. This would have been a familiar scene to anyone caught in the island campaigns of the Pacific. It is imagined the ship at left center is USS *The Sullivans* or that the image was photographed from *The Sullivans*. The explosions in the sky come from the 5-inch/38-caliber gun mounts as the first line of defense for Fletcher-class destroyers. There is a Japanese plane that splashed in the ocean, creating the column of water and debris at center. As the war progressed and US forces landed closer to the Japanese mainland, Japan's defensive tactics became more aggressive, concluding with kamikaze attacks. For the seizure and occupying campaigns for Iwo Jima and Okinawa, these aggressive tactics by the Japanese were on full display. USS *The Sullivans* was part of the screening fleet during these campaigns. In addition to shelling the island and beachheads, they would also stand at picket stations 10–15 miles away from the island, protecting the rest of the fleet from air, surface, and underwater threats.

The two wartime captains of USS *The Sullivans* are shown here. At left is the commissioning commander, Kenneth McLoud Gentry, who led the ship from September 30, 1943, to July 22, 1944. Below is the second captain of USS *The Sullivans*, Ralph Jacob Baum, listening to orders. He took command on July 22, 1944, until the end of the ship's service in World War II on September 19, 1945, when she was being fitted out at Mare Island. These two commanders guided USS *The Sullivans* successfully through the war. It is said that the five Sullivan brothers were protecting the ship, as she was never catastrophically hit by bombs, kamikazes, or shells. The ship only lost one sailor during her World War II years in one of the ship's watercraft, not onboard the ship herself.

One of the more harrowing months for USS *The Sullivans* was May 1945. The drive to and through Okinawa was in its second month, and kamikaze attacks against US Navy vessels were nearing their peak. One of the duties of the US destroyer was to rescue men from burning or sinking ships. These two images show USS *Bunker Hill* billowing smoke. Above, USS *The Sullivans* steams at full throttle, appearing to turn toward the stricken carrier. *Bunker Hill* was hit by two kamikazes at roughly the same time. Each dropped their bombs, creating secondary explosions, while the pilots crashed their planes into the flight deck. More than 400 men perished in these explosions. USS *The Sullivans* rescued and transported 166 men from the flight deck to the awaiting hospital ship, USS *Bountiful*. USS *Bunker Hill* returned home for repairs and was in dry dock when the war ended.

While this image does not have a description, the war diaries for USS *The Sullivans* record that the ship picked up 31 Japanese merchant seamen from the water on June 13, 1944, while screening the carriers USS *Bunker Hill*, USS *Wasp*, USS *Monterey*, and USS *Cabot*. These carriers and their picket destroyers comprised Task Group (TG) 58.2, which launched its air wings against Saipan and Tinian during the seizure and occupation campaign. These 31 men were classified as prisoners of war and were taken under guard to USS *Indianapolis* for transport to an unknown prison camp. The same day saw DD537 rescue a pilot, Ens. L.S. Mularski, attached to the aircraft carrier USS *Wasp*, from the water. Here, it appears that *The Sullivans* has pulled up alongside a watercraft and is in the process of hauling men and material aboard. As part of TG 58.2, USS *The Sullivans* was with her sister ships of Destroyer Division (DesDiv) 103 and DesDiv 104, both of which made up Destroyer Squadron (DesRon) 52.

Rough waves no doubt made this underway replenishment a bit harrowing for the deck and supply crew aboard USS *The Sullivans*. In this photograph, taken on January 10, 1945, when the ship arrived near Okinawa, an unknown oiler-supply auxiliary ship is conducting the operation with both *The Sullivans* and the USS *Astoria* (CL90) Cleveland-class cruiser. During her World War II service, DD537 was wearing the blue camouflage Measure 21, Navy Blue and Deck Blue. Behind the ship is the distinct profile of an Iowa-class battleship on the left and the partially obscured profile of another Fletcher-class destroyer, possibly from the same destroyer division as *The Sullivans*. Underway replenishments and the auxiliary ships that delivered them were lifelines to the fleet in the expanse of the Pacific Ocean, bringing fuel, food, mail, and other much-needed supplies.

Here are some of "Alleta's boys," as the Sullivan family referred to them. This image is like thousands of others from the wartime Navy. Men standing on the deck under the barrel of a mount or turret is a common sight. What makes this image unique is the man standing in the back at center. George Mendonsa was a quartermaster onboard USS *The Sullivans* and, after the war, went back home to Rhode Island to continue his work as a commercial fisherman. Based on a 2005 study at the Naval War College corroborated by the dean of the School of Arts at Yale University, Mendonsa is also known as "the kisser" in the famous Times Square photograph taken by Alfred Eisenstaedt. While there have been claims by many men to be the overjoyed male in the photograph, the Naval War College volunteer group and photograph experts concluded that George was most likely the kissing sailor due to verified scars and tattoos that are visible under close analysis.

Many who visit the Buffalo Naval Park ask where USS *The Sullivans* was when Japan unofficially surrendered on September 2, 1945. USS *The Sullivans* was scheduled for repairs and a refit in July 1945. Ordered for overhaul, she arrived at Mare Island, California, on July 9, 1945, where she was scheduled to remain until August 31. This photograph was taken after her refit in late August or early September. Some of the changes included the removal of one of her quintuple torpedo tubes between the funnels, the addition of twin 20mm guns, and the addition of the electronic countermeasure (ECM) antenna array on the aft superstructure. In the space vacated by the torpedo mount between the funnels, she carried two quadruple 40mms, one port and one starboard. She also had her paint scheme modified from Measure 21, overall blue, to Measure 22, the graded system, which is clearly evident here.

During the refit, sailors pose on the port bridge wing of DD537. Clearly shown is the Mark 37 gun director with the Mark 12 and 22 antennae at top. This gun director was the lead component of the Fletcher class's fire control system. During general quarters, it would be manned with up to five crew. They would track threats in the air and on the surface and send that data electronically to the gun plot computer. This Mark 1, and later the Mark 1A, fire control computer would input the data collated by the gun director. The analog computer would electronically pass that information to the 5-inch/38-caliber gun mounts and remotely move the mount to the target areas. Those manning the Mark 1 computer would also remotely fire the gun, though the mounts could retain local control as needed. Also shown is the scoreboard, or "kill board," of USS *The Sullivans*.

After the war, in January 1946, USS *The Sullivans* was decommissioned and added to the Pacific Reserve Fleet. A new conflict for the Cold War age, the Korean conflict, brought her back out of reserve in May 1951, and she was called again to duty. Recommissioned in July 1951 after a shakedown cruise to test ship and crew performance and to identify problems within her systems, she sailed on an "around the world" cruise, which lasted 217 days. Four months of that cruise were spent with Task Force 77, bombing the northern Korean peninsula and protecting the fleet from Soviet MiG attacks. The image to the right shows an underway replenishment or transfer during extremely heavy seas in 1952, while the image below shows Signalman C.F. Johnson raising the familiar shamrock flag after the ship's Korean War service. USS *The Sullivans* is sometimes called the "Flagship of the Irish Fleet."

Taken in 1958, these two images come from Tom Peter, a Buffalo native who sailed on USS *The Sullivans*. At left is the superstructure forward, Mount 51 and Mount 52, the bridge, the Mark 37 gun director, and the mainmast. As noted, one of the changes made during refits was the antenna on the Mark 37. In prior service, it carried the Mark 12 and 22, while here it shows the mesh and wire dish of the Mark 25. Also shown under the bridge wing are the ship's ribbons, which are still mounted in the same spot today. The image below shows a crewman in a rarely seen tropical white uniform on the quarterdeck, showing the painted shamrock. The emblem can currently be seen in the same spot. The two bracketed objects are the practice torpedo warheads for the Mark 14 torpedo mount. (Both, courtesy of the Peter family.)

Here are two images showing Tom and Alleta Sullivan greeting the crew of the ship and visiting a Navy hospital. Above, USS *The Sullivans* has just arrived home to the Philadelphia Shipyard from a cruise in the Mediterranean. Alleta, along with Tom and a now teenage Jimmy, son of Albert and Kathrine Mary, is holding a Battle "E" plaque awarded to the ship for efficiency in battle drills. Presenting it to them is Capt. James Nickerson. Below, Tom and Alleta shake hands with Seaman Sam Bass while greeting others at the Navy hospital at the Philadelphia Shipyard. Tom and Alleta worked tirelessly through all the years of DD537's service to stay close to the boys who served aboard her.

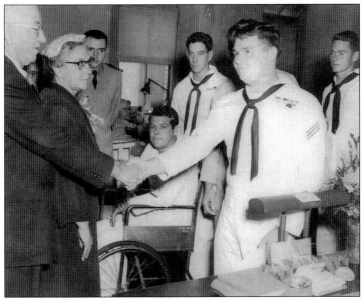

NY2-1460-8-52. USS THE SULLIVANS (DD537) BOW VIEW. ABOUT 45° RELATIVE.

Here are two views of the ship in the 1950s. The image above shows the peacetime camouflage of Ocean Gray, probably around the time of her around-the-world cruise for the Korean War. The refit from 1945 is still evident with the ECM array on the aft superstructure and the five 5-inch/38-caliber gun mounts. The image below was taken sometime after 1955. The ECM array has been moved forward near the aft funnel, and her Mount 53 5-inch/38-caliber gun mount has been removed on the aft superstructure to make way for the Mark 56 3-inch/50-caliber gun director, which can be seen at the top of the aft superstructure. This is the configuration USS *The Sullivans* is in today.

Unfortunately, the last time USS *The Sullivans* was in dry dock was in 1965, and these two images are evidence of that work. The ship was being decommissioned for the last time that year, and to prepare her for being out of commission in reserve, she was scraped and painted, and necessary repairs were made for the last time. The image above shows an aft quarter view of the starboard side with men on the scaffolds, while the picture below shows a close-up of the port side prop and shaft. The writing on the ship allows workers to see that the shaft was tested and filled. These shafts would be filled with oils and lubricants to keep them spinning smoothly, and the packing glands checked to make sure there was no seepage into the ship itself. Unfortunately, in the move in 2003 to the current location, the propellers were removed to account for the changes in the riverbed. This called for the need to fill the transom with water to keep her stern down. Losing the weight of the props required counterbalance, and water was the chosen ballast.

While the ship was in dry dock, the dockyard workers also made repairs to the main mast and the wide array of air and surface search radars and IFF (identification friend or foe) transponders. This image with the names of the equipment handwritten shows her postwar configuration. With changes to technology, and to the threats during the Cold War—jet aircraft and submarines—keeping an updated three-dimensional array was a necessity. Also shown are whip antennae for high-frequency (HF), very high frequency (VHF), and ultra-high frequency (UHF) radio communication. The most prominent arrays on USS *The Sullivans* today are the SPS 10 and SPS 6B. The SPS 10 was for conducting surface search, while the SPS 6B was for air search. Both of these radars were developed, tested, and added to US Navy vessels after World War II.

Most every ship in the US Navy has an association attached to it with "old salts" who served aboard. Sadly, many members from World War II–era ships have passed on, so these groups get smaller with the passage of time. These two images show reunions of the crew who served aboard. The upper image shows presumably the head table. Identified are George Mendonsa, the kissing sailor (center), along with Capt. Ira King, who was captain during her Korean service, on the left end of the table. This image is undated but was probably taken in the late 1950s or early 1960s. Below is a reunion here at the Buffalo Naval Park soon after the park opened, in 1979 or 1980. Reunions bring together the crew, their spouses, and sometimes their children to swap old stories and to help with upkeep on the ship. Sometimes, reunions carve out time for "working parties," where they help museum ships by volunteering their time for maintenance.

USS *The Sullivans* arrived in Buffalo on July 4, 1977, after a two-week trip through the St. Lawrence Seaway. USS *Little Rock* arrived on July 15, 1977, and local interest was evidenced by more than 3,000 people showing up for a ceremony celebrating their arrival. Both ships were docked here in Buffalo for two years, though not open to the public. Crowds would still gather to look at the ships from afar. The image above shows DD537 at her original berth, and at left is the Nitterauer family looking at the ship the day after her arrival. Those with a keen eye will notice that the port side is facing the pier, which means the ship is facing south. For about two months after the ship arrived, she faced this way until she was rotated to go "stern to bow" with USS *Little Rock*.

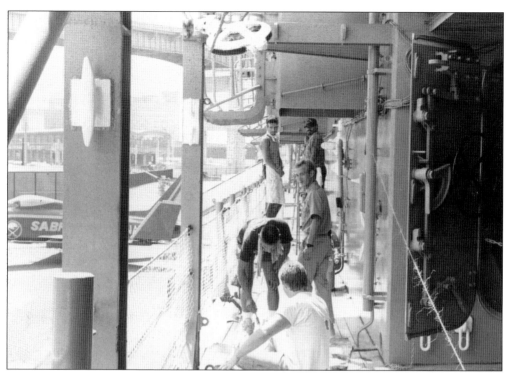

For two years, the ships were worked on and brought into some semblance of "ship-shape." With the opening of the Buffalo Naval Park in 1979, maintenance and preservation work continued. Every minute of every day, the ships are corroding, which brings water and weather into every section of the ship, from the top of the superstructures down to the keels. Here are two images of work being done on USS *The Sullivans* and USS *Little Rock* in the 1980s. At right, a volunteer paints the signal bridge (03) level of DD537, while above is a work crew on the main deck starboard on CLG4.

The legacy of the Sullivan family and the US Navy continued with the construction, commissioning, and active service of USS *The Sullivans* (DDG68), an Arleigh Burke–class destroyer. Here are two pictures of her commissioning in 1995. The ship was constructed at Bath Iron Works, now a subsidiary of General Dynamics, on the Kennebec River in Bath, Maine. There are currently 70 active ships of this class, with 12 more on order. These ships, ranging from 505 to 510 feet in length, use the Ageis combat system, the latest integrated guidance system to track and destroy enemy targets. Like the park's USS *The Sullivans*, the shamrock emblem is mounted on a funnel, and they fly the five-gold star battle flag.

Continuing her family's legacy of service and sacrifice, here is Kelly Sullivan christening the USS *The Sullivans* (DDG68) in 1995. As Jimmy Sullivan's daughter, she has taken acute pride in being a Sullivan. Like her great-grandmother Alleta before her in 1943, Kelly has a keen understanding of what both ships bearing her family's name means to America, the military, and the citizens they protect. Kelly speaks at great length about following in her great-grandmother's footsteps, using Alleta's model of what it means to be a good sponsor to a ship and the crew who serve aboard. Like Alleta, Kelly is engaged with her crew, visits the ship often when it is homeported in Florida, and spends time with the crew when they are on leave. Where Alleta wrote letters, Kelly communicates with them via email. DDG68 was put into commission in 1997 and has been serving America's interests since her shakedown cruise. The ship has been all over the world, from Japan to the Mediterranean ea, and has conducted exercises with NATO forces in the North Atlantic and the Persian Gulf. Recently, she was attached to the United Kingdom's Carrier Strike Group 21, with HMS *Queen Elizabeth*, the lead ship of British aircraft carriers.

USS *The Sullivans* is primarily a warship meant to bring violence to an enemy, but it is also home to the thousands of crew who served aboard her during her 22-year service history. The bonds between the crew are not broken with time or distance. They shared experiences many of us cannot imagine, and that experience keeps the crew together, even in death. USS *The Sullivans* represents a ship of sacrifice; the motto "We Stick Together" is a treasured sobriquet that guided the five Sullivan brothers, the crew while the ship was in service, and the Buffalo Naval Park's commitment to the ship. These two images show the crew during more relaxing times when the bonds of friendship were cultivated.

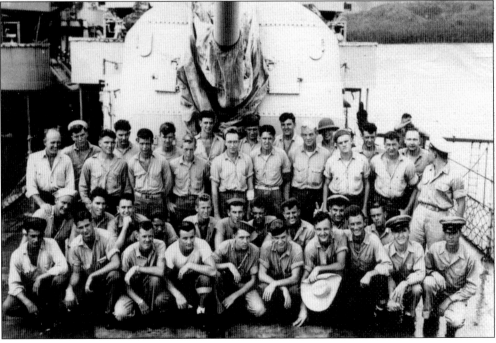

Four

USS CROAKER

FROM THE PACIFIC TO THE MED

A crewman on USS *Croaker* (SS246) hoists the battle flag, which proudly flies above the American ensign from the periscope. USS *Croaker* served America from 1944 to 1971, when she was finally taken out of service. Serving on submarines was on a volunteer basis and offered a completely different experience than serving on a surface vessel. It was a point of pride for a crewman to qualify for his "dolphins"—Submarine Warfare Insignia—by passing skill and knowledge tests while underway. Unlike surface vessels that may have 10 to 80 men doing one particular job, on a submarine, there may be only one or two. Crew who qualified had working knowledge of every system onboard in case they were called to man a station during general quarters that they did not rate for. A torpedoman would learn sonar or radio, and a machinist mate working in the engine room would have to know how to fire a torpedo. USS *Croaker* fulfilled its duty in the Pacific during World War II and the Cold War era of the 1950s and 1960s.

MRS. W. H. P. BLANDY
SPONSOR FOR THE
U.S. SUBMARINE CROAKER
DECEMBER 19, 1943
ELECTRIC BOAT CO. GROTON, CONN.

Here is the sponsor of USS *Croaker*, Roberta Blandy, wife of Adm. William Henry Purnell Blandy. The ship was christened on December 19, 1943, at the Electric Boat Company in Groton, Connecticut. Out of 77 Gato-class submarines, 41 were laid down at the Electric Boat Company. The remaining 36 were constructed at Portsmouth Naval Shipyard in Maine, Mare Island Naval Shipyard in California, and the Manitowoc Shipbuilding Company in Wisconsin. At left is *Croaker* going down the ways. The boat was commissioned and taken over by the US Navy on April 21, 1944.

Here is the partial crew attending the boat's party on April 15, 1944, at Polly's Inn in Norwich, Connecticut. This restaurant, no longer open, served as the main celebration facility for the boats that were constructed at the Electric Boat Company. There is a similar picture from USS *Cobia* (SS245)'s boat party, taken one month before on March 17, 1944, showing the same flags hanging from the ceiling. While 45 commissioning officers and crew are shown here for *Croaker*'s party, records indicate that when she steamed for Pearl Harbor in June 1944, there were 78 crew aboard, including eight officers and seven chief petty officers. A recent review of the crew roster and this image has allowed the Buffalo Naval Park's curator to identify 10 crew based on the stripes on the officers' sleeves and also the rate badges that can be seen on the arms of the chief petty officers and crew. The master of ceremonies for this party was L.E.B. Dauplaise, who is seventh from right in the last row. The answer to the question of whether these were the crew's and officer's wives, girlfriends, or sweethearts is lost to history.

Here are two more images from the party. Above is the officer's table. The first commander of the *Croaker*, Comdr. Jack Elwood Lee, is at right in the corner of the booth; below, he is cutting the cake. The woman in the polka-dot dress is presumably his wife, as she is near him in all three pictures. By this time in the war, Commander Lee had led USS *Grayling* (SS209) through seven successful war patrols, and had received his first of three Navy Crosses. After his orders came to proceed to Connecticut to take command of *Croaker*, USS *Grayling*, then commanded by Lt. Comdr. Robert M. Brinker, was lost with all hands on her next war patrol.

.. Special Menu ..

.. Special Menu ..

•

SHRIMP COCKTAIL

ROAST TOM TURKEY	BAKED SPICED HAM
STUFFED TOMATO LOAF	POTATO SALAD
TUNA SALAD	SLICED AMERICAN CHEESE
SALAMI	STUFFED EGGS

PICKLED EGGS

SWEET MIXED PICKLES	DILL PICKLES
STUFFED OLIVES	RIPE OLIVES
STUFFED CELERY HEARTS	PICKLED ONIONS
PICKLED PIG'S FEET	MAYONNAISE DRESSING
PREPARED MUSTARD	PREPARED RELISH

POTATO CHIPS

| PARKER HOUSE ROLLS | BREAD |

BUTTER

| LAYER CAKE | ICED CUP CAKES |

ASSORTED COOKIES

The Officers and Men of the U. S. S. Croaker
welcome their guests to the
ships party

L. B. E. DAUPLAISE, C. Q. M. (AA)
Master of Ceremonies

In the park's collection is an original ship's party pamphlet. The image above shows the inside of the pamphlet that was given to all the crew and guests. The right side shows the menu served that night of April 15. Historical menus can be found in many archival collections, and offer interesting insight into life at the time. They can be used to study what were considered delicacies at the time, along with names that may not be used today. The example of "Roast Tom Turkey" here is one of these. A "Tom Turkey" means a mature male turkey, a bird big enough to feed many people. To the right is a fun invitation poem created for the ship's party.

THE CONNECTICUT "CROAKERS"
OF NEW LONDON TOWN
INVITE YOU TO A PARTY
TO COME DOWN
PRIOR TO THE COMMISSIONING
OF THEIR BRAND NEW SHIP
BEFORE U. S. S. CROAKER
TAKES ITS INITIAL DEEP DIP
PLACE - IS NORWICH
AT INN OF POLLY
MEET APRIL 15, EIGHT-THIRTY
FOR FOLLY
SKIPPER - NONE OTHER
THAN OLE MAN LEE
SPONSOR - MRS. BLANDY
OUR HONOREE
NOW YOU'VE BEEN GIVEN
ALL THE DOPE
THAT YOU WILL COME
WE SINCERELY HOPE

Please present this card at the door

Shown are two images of USS *Croaker* in her early World War II configuration. The image above may show her during sea trials or her shakedown cruise. The boat's conning tower, radars, and typical armaments are incomplete and her hull number is not easily identified. Armaments and even conning tower designs changed through the course of World War II, as technology and threats changed. Many Gato-class submarines like USS *Croaker* started with a 3-inch/50-caliber gun mount on the deck, with 40mm and 20mm guns, but as the war carried on, many 3-inch/50-caliber gun mounts were changed out for the 4-inch/50-caliber gun or even, later in the war, to the 5-inch/25-caliber. The image below shows *Croaker* during service in late 1944 or 1945.

Taken during World War II, looking port side up to the bow, this photograph shows the conning tower and open fairwater lookout platform on USS *Croaker* at right. Early Gato-class submarines had an enclosed conning tower, which offered greater protection but created a much larger profile out of the water. It also reduced sight lines, as it was not fully open to the sky. The Navy, interested in trimming the profile of their subs while on the surface, created these more open conning towers, which can be seen on later boats of the class. Using this newer plan also allowed for armament to be shifted from the deck to the conning tower itself on certain subs. Radar also changed throughout the war, and mast configurations changed along with them. SD air-warning radars were used on all early fleet boats, and the addition of SJ radar continued to give American submarines a distinct advantage over the Japanese navy.

Here is USS *Croaker's* first kill going down by the stern on August 7, 1944. The Japanese light cruiser *Nagara* was the lead ship of the six Nagara-class cruisers. She was steaming to Nagasaki in a zig-zag pattern when at 11:00 that morning she was spotted by *Croaker*, which fired four stern torpedoes. Soon after, the ship took another tack, leading Captain Lee to believe the torpedoes would miss. Luckily, the ship turned again, and at 11:24, one torpedo struck. Below is a periscope photograph of a Japanese hospital ship. As described, it is presumed to be the *Titibana Maru*. In the *Croaker's* war diaries, it is noted on October 20, 1944, that they located a "properly identified Hospital ship" at 13,000 yards. Though the boat went to general quarters, Comdr. Jack Lee took photographs instead of torpedo shots, no doubt in a display of mercy and empathy.

AREA 11. JAPAN - GENERAL. Sortie CROAKER-2. Print #15, Roll B.
Shows Jap Hospital Ship, probably Titibana Maru taken at App. Lat.
32° 32' N. - Long. 127° 56' E, taken by the U.S.S. Croaker on the
2nd War Patrol. For data sheet covering this print, see ONI No.
370-208.   ONI (P-5) #370-209.

The Secretary of the Navy takes pleasure in commending the

UNITED STATES SHIP CROAKER

for service as follows:

"For outstanding heroism in action against enemy Japanese shipping and combatant units, during her First War Patrol in the East China and Yellow Seas from July 19 to August 31, 1944. Unrelenting, daring and tenacious, the U.S.S. CROAKER boldly penetrated a vigilant enemy air and surface screen to launch her deadly torpedoes which marked the doom of a valuable KUMA Class Cruiser. During subsequent aggressive night-surface attacks, she succeeded in destroying three additional enemy ships, including a freighter, a large tanker and a patrol vessel, for a total of 17,600 tons. The CROAKER's illustrious combat record attests the skill and gallant fighting spirit of her officers and men, and reflects the highest credit upon herself and the United States Naval Service."

All personnel attached to and serving on board the U.S.S. CROAKER during the above mentioned period are hereby authorized to wear the NAVY UNIT COMMENDATION Ribbon.

James Forrestal

Secretary of the Navy

Here is the Navy Unit Commendation for USS *Croaker*, Commander Lee, and her crew for action during her first war patrol from July 19 to August 31, 1944. The records indicate that the boat sank the cruiser *Nagara*, a small 2,000-ton freighter, a 500-ton patrol boat, and a large 10,000-ton oiler. With *Nagara* listed as 5,100 tons, the total tonnage for the war patrol was given as 17,600 tons. Also, this patrol was listed as "successful" for the Combat Insignia Award. During this first patrol, 15 members of the crew also qualified for their dolphins, completing the rigorous testing that comes with qualifying. After the war, the loss records of Japan were studied and compared to the US Navy's records. This gave a fascinating insight into what Japanese ships were lost, where, and when. The information was contrasted with which American submarine was in that patrol area during that period. The comparison between the two countries' records gave insight into the scoreboard embellishment that most American submarines undertook during the war. *Croaker's* total tonnage sunk during the war was downsized from 40,000 tons listed in the war diaries to 19,710 tons, though the number of vessels sunk stayed at 11.

USS *Croaker* ended her war service on August 22, 1945, while standing on lifeguard duty in the South China Sea and Hong Kong area. During this war patrol, they had no opportunities to rescue any American pilots or to inflict damage on the enemy. USS *Croaker* might not be docked at the Buffalo Naval Park if the aerial bomb that damaged her superstructure was not a dud. During her fifth war patrol, on May 30, 1945, she attacked and sank two small coastal oilers and a patrol craft for a total of 5,800 tons while taking the damage seen here. When the war ended, she sailed for Galveston, Texas, and then back to Groton, Connecticut, to be put into reserve. But that was not the end of her service. As with USS *The Sullivans* and USS *Little Rock*, the crew developed friendships and camaraderie that lasted lifetimes. In total, roughly 260 US submarines took part in World War II. They accounted for the sinking of 1,400 ships totaling over five million tons. The victory came at a high cost for the US "silent service," as 52 boats were lost—roughly 20 percent of all submarines.

After being out of commission in reserve at New London, Connecticut, as part of the Atlantic Reserve fleet, *Croaker* was brought back as a training ship in 1951 and underwent a conversion from April to December 1953 and was recommissioned SSK246. While still a Gato-class submarine, the Hunter-Killer submarine conversion added the "K" to her designation. With the world order shifting after World War II, and the Soviet Union becoming the greatest threat to America, the US government was shocked to learn that the military buildup of the Soviet Union included 300–400 submarines, most of the Whiskey class. To bring submarines of the World War II era up to speed, the Navy created various programs for remaining Gato submarines. These two images show USS *Croaker* in her hunter-killer (SSK) conversion.

Here is USS *Croaker* pulling into Malta in 1965. The tiny republic, located between Sicily and the coast of Africa, was a major Allied port during World War II, and won its independence from the United Kingdom in 1964. *Croaker's* conversion kept her relevant on the world stage until 1971. In total, seven Gatos followed the SSK conversion. One of the most important roles was the need to track enemy submarines, a fundamentally and drastically different duty for submarines from what they had done up to that point. To that end, the BQR-4 sonar was mounted on the nose of the boat. This lessened noise interference from the boat itself while extending the sonar's range. Inside, one of the four diesel-electric engines was removed to create space for the sonar and new radar equipment while having the secondary effect of also creating a quieter boat. USS *Croaker* spent much of her second life participating in NATO's anti-submarine exercises in the North Atlantic and patrolling the Mediterranean with the US Sixth Fleet.

Here is a view of USS *Croaker* pulling into Port Hercules, Monaco, in 1956. In the background on the hilltop is Prince Rainier and Princess Grace's home, while to the right of *Croaker* is a craft with a little more luxury—Aristotle Onassis's yacht *Christina*. Guiding *Croaker* into the port are the two lighthouses that bookended the old port from the 1920s to the 2000s. It was on this trip that Princess Grace stepped aboard USS *Croaker* to invite the captain and officers to a wedding. The deck crew can be seen preparing the boat for docking.

The only cruise book for USS *Croaker* in the park's collections is from the 1963 Mediterranean cruise. Nicknamed "Tigris Mediterraneus," or "Tiger of the Med," USS *Croaker* steamed 15,032 miles and visited nine ports of call from July 16, 1963, to November 2, 1963. Leaving from New London, this would be the third time in her career she would be attached to the US Sixth Fleet. Above, the crew is getting some much-needed sun and fresh air on the forward deck. On the port side is the BQR-3A hydrophone, while on starboard the portable torpedo derrick and T-brace for lowering torpedoes can be seen. The image below shows a commissaryman second class in the cramped galley.

This fascinating photograph, also from the 1963 *Croaker* cruise book, shows a periscope image of USS *Little Rock* from *Croaker* during training exercises. Neither crew could have had any idea that the two vessels would be docked next to each other in Buffalo decades later. The location of this image is not known, other than the Mediterranean, but in addition to CLG4, *Croaker* put under her sights USS *Independence* (CVA62), USS *Saratoga* (CVA60), USS *Long Beach* (CGN9), USS *Hardwood* (DDE861), and USS *Borie* (DD704). Exercises like this would take place both during the day and at night to test the mettle and endurance of US submarine commanders and crew. From 1962 to 1965, USS *Little Rock* was attached to the Sixth Fleet, serving as the flagship in 1962. She again returned to the Mediterranean in 1967 to continue her duty carrying the admiral's flag.

The *Croaker* housed thousands of men within her pressure hull across her years of service. In World War II, men came aboard fresh from training centers and spent their free time during war patrols qualifying for their dolphins. In her six World War II patrols, 71 men earned their dolphins while serving. The image at left shows a corpsman petty officer first class during a swearing-in ceremony. He is proudly displaying his dolphins on his left breast. Below, USS *Croaker* delivers "Mercy Missiles" to an unknown country. Two submarines, USS *Croaker* and USS *Archerfish*, are known to have delivered goods to welfare organizations around the world for the Navy League during the late 1950s and early 1960s.

Here are two images of the USS *Croaker's* crew. Above is a view of the aft engine room showing two machinist mates sitting at the door that leads to the maneuvering room, which controlled the electrical plant. This image was given to the naval park by the crewman at left. Unfortunately, no names are listed on the photograph. The image below shows the crew during the boat's 1965 dry dock in Kittery, Maine. By this time in *Croaker's* service, many of the crew shown here would continue their careers in nuclear submarines.

After being stricken from the Naval Register in 1971, USS *Croaker* began her life as a museum ship where she was constructed, in Groton, Connecticut. This brochure is from her time as a museum ship from 1977 to 1987, when the US Navy reclaimed her because of deterioration and neglect. Today, the Navy possibly would have reefed the boat or sold her for scrapping. Thankfully, she was again offered to museums and naval parks around the country. The City of Buffalo applied and was awarded the right to be the new home for *Croaker*. This fulfilled a multi-year mission of the park to secure a submarine. Since the park's inception and founding, the first goal was to secure a submarine, and its target in 1976 was USS *Becuna* (SS319), a Balao-class submarine. Eventually, USS *Becuna* found a home worthy of her World War II and Cold War service at the Independence Seaport Museum in Philadelphia, where she resides today next to USS *Olympia* (protected cruiser C6).

Here is *Croaker* in "as-is" condition when she arrived in Buffalo. The deterioration along the superstructure is obvious in this port side image. Looking at her conning tower, a noticeable lack of antenna arrays is evident. Missing are her No. 1 and No. 2 periscopes, snorkel induction, electronic countermeasures antenna and stub mast, and IFF, UHF, VLF, and AN/BRA antennas. While the Buffalo Naval Park received positive support during her arrival, a cartoon expressed the feelings of some in the Western New York area. Tom Toles, a Pulitzer Prize–winning editorial cartoonist who worked at the *Buffalo News* at the time, drew this cartoon expressing his beliefs.

A thorough survey of the submarine was conducted when she arrived. The image above shows one of the torpedo tubes half full of water, with a thin layer of ice on top. The park has an extensive collection of survey photographs, offering a unique insight into the condition of the boat upon arrival. Evidence shows there were trees beginning to grow in the superstructure, and water incursion was prevalent. Below is one of the General Motors V16 diesel engines that connected to electric generators to power the shafts and propellers, while also charging the two batteries onboard.

Above is a view of one of the two engine rooms. Since US submarines during World War II did not have snorkel technology to run their diesels underwater, two batteries—each with 126 cells—were used to power the boat while submerged. While this technology only allowed for a dive of three to ten hours, it was long enough to hide from enemy planes and destroyers. Below is a good view of the outside of the pressure hull. In World War II, American submarines were double hulled, with a pressure hull, which contained the compartments where the crew lived, and an outer hull, which contained the ballast and fuel tanks. In the forward and aft torpedo rooms, toward the tapered ends, only the outer hull was present.

As with the park's other vessels, the men who served aboard formed a brotherhood that is not easily broken. Above, near the end of her career in 1968, the USS *Croaker's* crew and officers pose for a picture on the deck. Holding the banner on the left is the last commander, Comdr. Bob Hurley. The *Croaker* successfully served American interests for 25 years, bringing skill and a little luck to the Japanese ships she sunk in the 1940s and the Russian subs she tracked during the Cold War. The image below shows a serene moment as *Croaker's* bow points toward Mount Suribachi on the conquered island of Iwo Jima at daybreak on May 5, 1945. During her first war patrol, the crew welcomed Lt. Comdr. R.B. Lakin from the British navy. Lakin said in his report to the admiralty, "The attention and interest shown to him [Lakin] and the great consideration for his comfort and welfare displayed by the officers and men of USS *Croaker* made it a great pleasure to be allied with such excellent messmates during this fine patrol."

Five

WESTERN NEW YORK
SACRIFICES AND RESOURCEFULNESS

Buffalo and Western New York answered the call of President Roosevelt to switch America's production and manufacturing of goods and services to the production of war materiel. Under the creation of the War Production Board, America went from building cars and appliances to tanks, planes, guns, and ships. Houde Engineering, on East Delavan Avenue in Buffalo, switched from making hydraulic shock absorbers for cars and trains to producing hydraulic retracting cylinders for various war equipment. Seen here are "Rosie the Riveters" at the assembly station adding caps to the cylinders. The company grew during the war years, and at its peak employed 2,800 workers during World War II.

These two sailors represent Buffalo's connection to the light cruiser USS *Juneau*. While the ship is known for the Sullivan brothers and the Rogers brothers from Connecticut, an additional 675 crewmen went down with her on November 13, 1942. Unfortunately, two of those crew were from Buffalo. At left is Jerry Reilly, who had a hard upbringing in South Buffalo. He enlisted at 17 and rated a gunner's mate onboard USS *Juneau* after serving a stint on USS *Brooklyn*. Below is Edmund Mozgawa, who came from Lackawanna, New York. He perished aboard the ship the day after his 19th birthday.

Curtiss-Wright was one of the largest employers in Buffalo and Western New York during World War II. The above image shows some of the office workers, including Dorothy Bender, marked "Mom" at left, in the plant near the corner of Kenmore Avenue and Vulcan Street. Curtiss-Wright had two main assembly plants and other metal production plants throughout Buffalo. At right is Mitzi Ziegler-Ferster, who was a nose cone inspector at one of the plants during the war.

These two images show the most well-known products of the Curtiss-Wright Company. Above is a P-40 Warhawk, produced at both assembly plants in Buffalo. A total of 13,500 P-40s were assembled during the war years. In addition, over 2,000 C-46 Commando transport aircraft were rolling off the assembly lines at the same time. Below is one of the most famous aircraft of World War I, the Curtiss JN-4 "Jenny." These biplanes were mass-produced as training aircraft for US Navy and US Army pilots and continued their prevalence after the war, as many were sold as private civilian aircraft. Hundreds were produced at the now-demolished plant on Elmwood Avenue in North Buffalo.

Along with the Curtiss-Wright plants, the Bell Aircraft Corporation was founded in Buffalo by executives of Consolidated Aircraft Company after Consolidated moved to California. The largest plant was in Wheatfield, New York, outside Niagara Falls. At this plant, shown in both images, over 13,000 P-39 Airacobras and P-63 Kingcobras were produced for the war effort. Above is a bird's-eye view, while the below image shows part of the aircraft assembly line.

The image above shows the streamlined profile of two P-39 Airacobras, while below, a crew stands around one at the Laurel Army Airfield in Laurel, Mississippi. At this base, the Airacobras were used to train army pilots. The unique design of the Airacobras and Kingcobras was designed to meet Lawrence Bell's desire for a "cannon on wings." He wanted these planes to be the most heavily armed aircraft in the country. That meant moving the engine to the middle of the craft underneath and behind the pilot, giving the nose the space to carry a 50-caliber machine gun and its ammunition.

As the banner indicates, the 10,000th fighter craft rolled off the assembly line with Lawrence Bell, president of Bell Aircraft, standing at left. After this image was captured, Bell produced about 3,000 more aircraft before the end of World War II. The impact of having Bell and Curtiss-Wright headquartered in Niagara Falls and Buffalo at that time can be measured in many ways. The growth of Western New York's middle class was in no small part due to these two companies and the associated plants and factories that subsequently opened to feed their assembly lines. At the peak of war production, the companies employed 81,000 workers combined. After the war, each plant scaled back production and moved on to other projects. Bell Aircraft developed helicopters and the X-1, which Chuck Yeager used to break the sound barrier. Eventually, Bell moved its headquarters to Texas. Curtiss-Wright moved to Ohio in 1946, asserting that the plants used to build the P-40 and C-46 were too large to remain profitable.

Above is another large factory in Buffalo that made products for the war effort. The Buffalo Forge Company produced blowers and air movers for the US Navy. All Cleveland-class cruisers, like the USS *Little Rock*, had Buffalo Forge blowers and air movers integrated into their design. Below is a manufacturing stamp from Worthington Pump Company. While headquartered in New Jersey, its Buffalo plant was the largest subsidiary, with 1,800 employees spread across 72 buildings. This stamp was taken out of the evaporator compartment on the third deck of USS *Little Rock* and put on display. The feed pump was installed on USS *Little Rock* during her construction in 1943 or 1944.

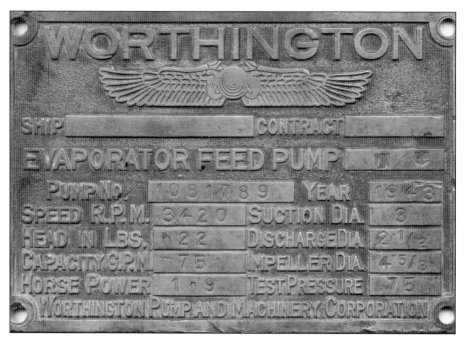

To the right is the brochure created for the Army-Navy "E" Award celebration for Linde Air Products Company's Buffalo plant. Below is a celebration given for the Spenser Lens Company, a subsidiary of American Optical Company, held at Kleinhans Music Hall. The two companies earned a combined 12 "E" Awards for excellence in manufacturing and production. The army and navy were both eager to recognize companies that exceeded production goals while maintaining safe environments. Issued by both the undersecretary of war and of the navy, companies would be subject to review and, if qualified, would first receive a pennant. If subsequent visits every six months proved satisfactory, the company would receive a star it could place on the pennant. In total, 79 companies throughout Western New York received a combined 260 "E" awards.

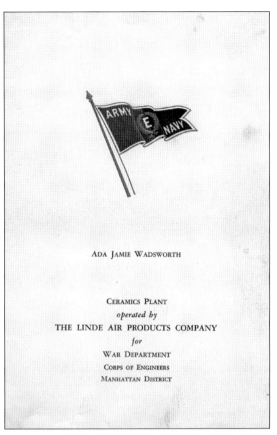

ADA JAMIE WADSWORTH

CERAMICS PLANT
operated by
THE LINDE AIR PRODUCTS COMPANY
for
WAR DEPARTMENT
CORPS OF ENGINEERS
MANHATTAN DISTRICT

The park's artifact collection is filled with images of men from Buffalo and Western New York who served fearlessly with the 8th and 15th Army Air Corps. The image above shows 1st Lt. John O'Brien kneeling at center. He served as a bomber in the 8th Army Air Corp headquartered in England. At left is a picture taken by him on a bombing run over Germany. As would be expected of the 8th Army Air Corp, the bombers are the B-17 Flying Fortress. Heated debates over day or night bombing took place between the Allies, with America agreeing to daylight bombing while Great Britain took over nighttime bombing raids.

Another Buffalo native, Bill Hess, was attached to the 15th Air Corps 455th Bomber Group based in Italy. The 455th conducted 252 bombing missions, hitting military and production targets throughout northern Italy, Czechoslovakia, and southern Germany. Above, Hess is kneeling second from right. Below is a close-up of the nose art and scoreboard of his bomber *Tepee Time Gal*. As the Axis powers retreated, the Allies were able to establish a foothold closer to Axis home territories. These movements allowed the bombers to reach their targets more easily, bringing a swifter end to the war.

"RUHR
GERMAN

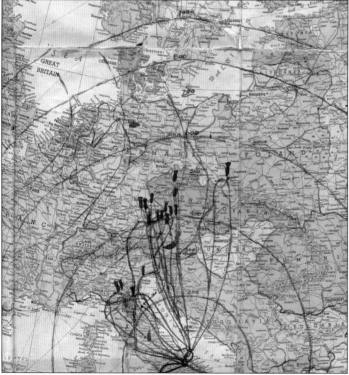

At left is an original bombing map made by Bill Hess during or after the war. It shows the missions that *Tepee Time Gal* flew while he was part of the crew, with their airstrip in Italy at the bottom. The photograph above shows multiple bombers, above and below, maneuvering through anti-aircraft flak above Ruhr, Germany. While this image came from Hess's collection, according to his map, *Tepee Time Gal* never bombed the Ruhr region, which borders western Germany.

114

WAGNER   TAYLOR   BUDTRSZK OSBURN
                    MURPHY
                                    CYMERMAN

More images from the collections of Buffalo bomber crewmembers are seen here. At right is a top-down view of B-24 Liberators taken by a Sergeant Klein over Germany. Klein was attached to the 15th Air Corps that flew missions from Italy, along with *Tepee Time Gal.* Above, Alois Cymerman kneels at far right with the rest of the flight crew of the B-17 Liberator *Swing Shift.* Cymerman was a radio operator and flew 51 missions before the war's end. The Buffalo Naval Park has his bomber jacket on display featuring the nose art of his plane—a blond woman on a swing— painted on the back.

CT 528, launched in August, 1943, at Bison Shipyard

Here is the same LCT 528 after hitting the Normandy Coast during the invasion

The Bison Shipbuilding Company, located on Tonawanda Island north of Buffalo, was a World War II shipyard that built LCTs (Landing Craft, Tank). While an unprecedented number of ships were built on the coasts during the war years, many companies around the Great Lakes were producing ships too. Bison Shipbuilding produced the most LCTs for the war effort, a total of 360. They were 114 to 120 feet in length and 32 feet at the beam. Their displacement fully loaded was 280 tons. Bison Shipbuilding first began building them to meet British requests in 1942. The image at left shows an LCT hitting the water for the first time (top) and later on the beaches of Normandy during the Allied invasion. Below are some of the Bison Shipbuilding employees.

Here are two images from the Buffalo Naval Park collections that highlight nurses. Above is Sylvia Koller, who was from Buffalo. She attended Nardin Academy, a private girls' high school, and went on to join the US Navy. During World War II, she was appointed chief nurse on the USS *Tranquility* (AH14), an 800-bed hospital ship that joined the Pacific fleet in May 1945. Even though the war was nearing its conclusion, the *Tranquility* was the base hospital for the summer at Ulithi, where they rescued survivors from USS *Indianapolis*. In the months after the war, Koller continued her service, transporting patients back to America. Pictured at right is Raphaela Picucci (left), a nurse during World War II, at Fort Devens in Massachusetts. Though Picucci was not from Buffalo originally, she settled here after the war.

At right is Kay Jiambra, a Buffalo native who was one of 83,000 American women to enlist in the Women Accepted for Volunteer Emergency Service (WAVES) branch of the US Navy. She was rated a photographer's mate and is seen here developing photographs for the war effort. The WAVES program, part of the US Navy Reserve, was implemented with the mission of bringing on women to work stateside, releasing men to go to the combat zones. Passed into law on July 30, 1942, the program's main training facility for enlisted women was at Hunter College in the Bronx, New York. Once this six-week training was completed, 16 colleges and universities around the country were chosen as specialized schools to train the graduates in their specific job duties. Like the traditional US Navy, the WAVES also had 8,000 women officers. Programs like the WAVES and SPAR (Coast Guard), WAC (Army), and WASP (Air Force) paved the way for future gender and racial integration into all branches of the US military.

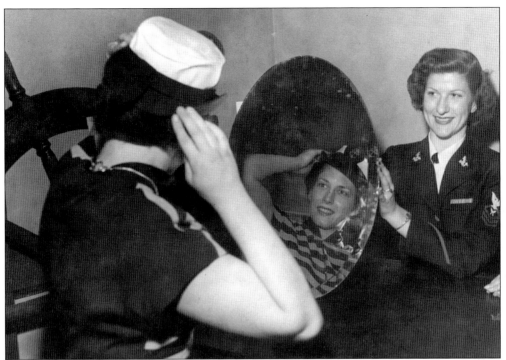

Dolores Schulenberg was a WAVES recruiter from the Buffalo area. During World War II, she recruited in eastern Pennsylvania and the Philadelphia area for the program. After the war, she continued to serve America as a recruiter, coming back home to Buffalo to take on similar duties in Western New York. She served as a WAVES recruiter through the Korean War up until 1955, and retired as a chief petty officer. Above, she is enticing Dorothy Lake to join by letting her try on the brimmed cap worn by a WAVE. Below, Schulenberg sits with three potential recruits from the Olean, New York, area south of Buffalo.

Sixty-five years separate these two images of submarines with very different histories. Above is USS *Buffalo* (SSN715). The nuclear submarine was the second naval vessel named for the city, though three ships were planned as USS *Buffalo* during World War II but never commissioned. This USS *Buffalo* was constructed at the Newport News Shipbuilding Company in Virginia and commissioned in 1983. She spent most of her 35-year career attached to the Western Pacific Fleet, conducting missions vital to national security. She was decommissioned in 2019 and is currently being dismantled. The image to the left is unique, as it shows a World War I German submarine that surrendered to the Allies at the end of hostilities. The 1919 photograph shows her docked at the foot of Main Street in Buffalo as part of a tour of the Great Lakes. UC97, a coastal minelaying sub, was constructed at the end of the war and never saw action.

The USS *Harold J. Ellison* was a Gearing-class destroyer commissioned in June 1945. Her namesake was from Buffalo and was part of the doomed Torpedo Squadron 8 attached to the USS *Hornet* during the Battle of Midway. The aviators shown in this image, except for Ens. George Gay, did not survive the battle, and all were presumed dead on June 5, 1942. Flying without cover in obsolete Douglas TBD Devastators, all 15 planes of the squadron were shot down without scoring any torpedo hits on the Japanese fleet. While the men gave their lives in an unsuccessful attack, they inadvertently diverted the attention of the Japanese navy's 1st Carrier Strike Force, allowing for the successful dive-bombing missions that were to come later in the battle. At the end of the day, the Japanese had lost all four of their carriers engaged in the battle and were stopped in their advance to overtake the island of Midway, an American stronghold. Standing third from right is Harold Ellison. Aboard the USS *Little Rock*, the Buffalo Naval Park has a compartment dedicated to Ellison, along with a model of the destroyer named for him.

There are hundreds of servicemen and women honored at the Buffalo Naval Park. Two servicemen prominent to the park's mission are Pfc. William J. Grabiarz and 2nd Lt. John P. Bobo. Grabiarz (left), from Buffalo, and Bobo (below), from Niagara Falls, were both posthumously awarded the Medal of Honor for meritorious action in World War II and Vietnam, respectively. Grabiarz used his body as a shield to protect his troop commander, while Bobo held a defensive position against a larger enemy force so his command group could gain protection against an ambush. Grabiarz was 19, and Bobo was 24. Both were brought back to Western New York for burial. The selfless deeds of these two men are central to the story at the Buffalo Naval Park, and their stories are used to educate, honor, inspire, and preserve.

Six

CAPSIZE!

WHAT HAPPENED AND THE WAY FORWARD

The dominating news at the Buffalo Naval Park in 2022 was the capsizing of the Fletcher-class destroyer USS *The Sullivans*. Her celebrated career as an active warship is discussed in chapter three of this book. She represents the largest wartime loss of life of any American family while also memorializing all Gold Star families. Both ships that carry the name USS *The Sullivans* proudly fly the five–gold star flag, the same flag that adorned the window of the Sullivan home at 98 Adams Street in Waterloo, Iowa.

For 45 years, Buffalo Naval Park has been the caretaker of the ship and her story. The park's staff, past and present, has a profound understanding of the importance of the ship. The staff has also worked hard under the ever-present limitations of human and financial resources that plague all museum ships. While the capsizing happened over the course of 12 hours, the events leading up to it did not happen overnight.

On April 13, 2022, park staff noticed that the ship was taking a starboard list. The weather during the day was windy, the water in the Buffalo River was up three to four feet, and the ship's caretaker was asked to monitor the situation. The author and one other staff member worked late into the evening, and as they were leaving for the night, the list grew more profound and startling. They immediately called the director of operations and the maintenance foreman, who came down to the ship and went below decks. At that moment, they knew it was too late. They immediately put in calls to a salvage company they had used in the past and waited for a response. By 8:45 a.m. on April 14, the ship had settled onto the riverbed at about a 20-degree list. One hour later, she had resettled into a 35-degree list and remained there for the rest of the incident.

The park's leadership—the president and CEO, along with the board of directors—assembled a team comprising the US Coast Guard, Bidco (a local marine company), T&T Salvage from Texas, the City of Buffalo, the New York State Department of Environmental Conservation, Miller Environmental, Abbey Mecca (a marketing agency), Buffalo Fire, and Buffalo Police. This team of experts came together under the overall leadership of the Coast Guard.

The most immediate need was to make sure the ship was stabilized and would not be a threat to the workers who would need to move about her. Second was the need to find any holes in the hull and seal them, preventing any further water incursion. In addition, there was a need to contain the 40,000 gallons of oil and diesel fuel onboard before they could leak into the river. Three daily meetings were held—at 7:00 a.m., noon, and 4:00 p.m.

The ship was designed with the ability to flex and twist, with expansion joints running through transverse bulkheads, but an unorganized pumping plan could have strained the ship beyond those limits and it could have easily been lost. After weeks of test pumping and data analysis, it was decided that once pumping began it would occur in three stages, and the ship was divided into three zones. Zone A was the bow and platforms in front of the forward engine room; zone B was the four machinery compartments, the two fire rooms, and two engine rooms, which contained the most water; and zone C was the aft section of the ship behind the aft engine room. Each zone had different amounts of water. Zone B would be pumped first until it had roughly the same amount of water as zone C. Then the pumps in zone C would be turned on, and zones B and C would be pumped down in conjunction until they both had the same amount of water as zone A, at which time all three zones would be pumped out simultaneously. Once the pumping began, within hours the ship had been sealed, righted, and stabilized. She had made it out of the ordeal.

Next, working closely with a local conservator, a disaster plan was laid out and a volunteer program was enacted to assess the condition of the artifacts onboard. Everything was removed and placed on the decks of the ships to dry out. Anything beyond conservation or preservation was cataloged and disposed of. In total, about 65–70 percent of the donated artifacts were preserved and re-cataloged. The tragedy provided the Buffalo Naval Park with a clean slate to remake the ship following preservation and furnishing guidelines laid out for historic vessels.

As the spring became summer, the incident remained on the park staff's minds. They knew that while DD537 was out of immediate danger, she was not in the clear yet. A winter emergency plan was created, while outreach to naval architects brought the park together with a prominent surveyor who spent weeks collecting data on the ship's current condition and providing recommendations. Plans such as dry docking or coffer damning are being discussed, along with budget development and advocacy plans to help pay for them.

The Buffalo Naval Park has been truly grateful to US senator Chuck Schumer and to New York state legislators who have provided funding to help the park. The support of the local, national, and international community, including the Sullivan family and local business leaders, has been second to none and has given the staff the strength to carry on. Other museum ships around the country have also fully supported the park, and the Historic Naval Ships Association has been present every step of the way. The park staff shares their hard lessons learned to all museums that ask.

Today, the ship has been righted and stabilized. In the six weeks of the capsizing, 58 holes were plugged, and two large gashes of four feet and ten feet were temporarily sealed. It is believed that these gashes are what started the capsize. Over a period of 13 hours, the ships had been hit with three seiches (quickly rising water pushed by wind from Lake Erie) that raised and lowered the ships to such extremes that USS *The Sullivans* hit the bottom of the riverbed, which crinkled and perforated the hull plating, creating the gashes.

The numbers tell the story: 40,000 gallons of oil and diesel fuel and 1.2 million gallons of water were contained and pumped out, yet scores of ship artifacts and donated items were lost. This event is now part of the service history of USS *The Sullivans*, and the story of her capsizing will be added to the park's collections along with her war diaries, crew letters, and logs. For the staff of the Buffalo Naval Park, the most important number is one—one ship has been saved.

The morning of April 14, 2022, showed how USS *The Sullivans* settled throughout the night. This photograph was taken as she stabilized for a few hours. Shortly after, another seiche swelled into the Buffalo River, lifting the ship and resettling her further into the Buffalo River. The starboard depth charge rack still has her full complement of depth charges. After the final settling, those depth charges came loose and were floating in the water.

This startling image shows the ship's roughly 35-degree list after she settled into her final position. Not only did staff worry about the condition of the ship below the waterline, but everything above decks like the deck houses, superstructure, tripod mast, and ECM antennae were being closely monitored. There was great concern that having these structures in this position for a long time would snap the welds, shift equipment, and break off parts of the ship that were untouched by the water. The trailers on the promenade are the pumps that were brought to the scene to begin the pumping-out process. At left is a very welcome sight to all first responders, staff, and others involved with the incident. The USS *The Sullivans* lives again to tell her story.

DESTROYER 537
IEM STEELCO. SHIPBUILDING DIVISION
HULL 5379
1943   SAN FRANCISCO YARD
3   OFFICIAL PHOTO SPONSOR'S GROUP
O BE RELEASED FOR PUBLICATION

Your first temptation, when the news comes, is to lock your door and retire into your own private grief. You want to sit alone in your room and cry your heart out. You want to bar the well-meaning friends who come to your house trying to help, and, above all, to close the door against the reporter and writers who want to talk to you about those you loved. I hope that *The Sullivans* will make other people more conscious of the importance of working, giving, living, and, if need be, dying to make our country live. In that way, my five boys will still be fighting.

—Alleta Sullivan, *The American Magazine*, March 1944.

Discover Thousands of Local History Books Featuring Millions of Vintage Images

Arcadia Publishing, the leading local history publisher in the United States, is committed to making history accessible and meaningful through publishing books that celebrate and preserve the heritage of America's people and places.

Find more books like this at
www.arcadiapublishing.com

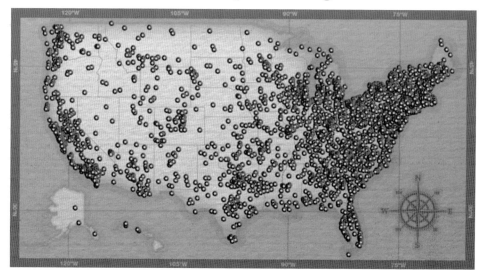

Search for your hometown history, your old stomping grounds, and even your favorite sports team.

Consistent with our mission to preserve history on a local level, this book was printed in South Carolina on American-made paper and manufactured entirely in the United States. Products carrying the accredited Forest Stewardship Council (FSC) label are printed on 100 percent FSC-certified paper.

MADE IN THE USA